The Silent Fathom

The Silent Fathom

By Ramia Sorayya Moss

Designed by Ramia Sorayya Moss

ISBN 9798840844731

Table of Contents

The Mouth

Silent life, the sound of the birth of all.
Sound, the mouth of the universe.
But rivers flow south into the Mississippi,
And time is now, and time will still remain.
Though you stand tall before the frosted oak,
The silence of its growth deafens your strength.

I said one day that we would be wed.
And, yea, it has been settled in the solid destiny
That silence has written.

And, yes, I will sorrow forgive.
And I will sorrow forgive.

Form

We perform the dance of form,
A teleological phenomenon,
A reason to speak of life.
Ah, the gestation period of creation is water.
And as it goes, we were
Bacteria to life to beast to man to love to poet-
ry.
I was once a field of viola tricolor, atop a field
of bodies,
Blood bath, soldiers remorse.
The fathoms of time continue, the seasons
pay no heed.
Do you know the wind?
It's cold and unforgiving in the North.
And synonyms of love and pleasure
Are weakness and time.

Angels

Angels are light on a prison wall.
They chant, in unknown languages,
Whispering of holiness.
I have become the Light, the Way, and the
Vine.
There is laughter on a subway train, the mind
betrays.
My mind is a valley, and a fawn runs
through, timid and afraid.
What is chasing the fawn?
It's a thought, dark and drawn out, and then
fleeting away.
I am the way.

Freedom in a Nation

The only remedy for freedom is a dark night
of the taming of the soul.
The soil bleeds tulips, ready for the taking.
The father of the nation speaks boldly of the
tide,
And the narrow minds of the people
Listen. Listen to the hum of the radiophonic
syllables.
What is this restless wind in the trees?
I believe it's my mother, dying little by little.
I believe it's my daughter, buried and gone.
And only the change that wipes out a youth,
Only the winter, who symbolizes equilibri
um,
Only they can save me now,
From freedom.
And someday maybe I will migrate to a land
Where freedom cannot destroy me.

I Have Said Good-bye

Your love exited as quickly as it came,
A diamond, worn on the breast of royalty,
A remorse, a new and shining stone, sunlit,
resplendent and new.
I have said good-bye to the wind,
And the rain plummets over Grand Rapids.
The rain on the river, the sky is wild and un-
predictable.
Oh, have you seen a light?
It's water lily.
The stone on my finger is washed and your
face is dim in a pool of memory.
I have said good-bye to the wind, and the
rain, and the cloud of matrimony.

Lover

Frost covers the windshield, I see, and at an arm's length, a child,
My winter's blue.
I have taken the day as an enemy.
And my sorrow is looming in the twilight.
Hemlock lies dormant in the soil,
And I am taken with the dark lily
Pushing its slender stalk through the damp earth,
A memory of love's hand.
Do not grieve for me,
There are starry emblems in my eyes
Where my lover lost his sweet gaze.
There's night in my hair, and I'm taken with fever.
Dark, dark sky,
I'm witched,
Waiting to leave this town.
He will come and take us away,
He is the looming storm on the shifting horizon.
His soft gesture
Will fill our lives with
Clouds pregnant with the rains of glory.

The Wind

I have said good-bye to the wind.
The desert's sky, the dangerous stars and the drum of Africa.
The Moroccan home to
Those who take, eat, and bind with love
Is not mine.

In this small town,
A home, my house is a fable.
There are tulips in the garden,
A musical anthem to the working class.
I am a white rose, I'm a feather floating in the wind beneath the sky's deaf height.

Can the sky remember those who worshiped
Amongst my ancestors?
They stood on this land,
The miracle of a seedling.
The miracle of a plant bursting in their souls.

And now, though, what would they think if I said good-bye to the wind?
And the rain will
Wash away the heavens and the earth.
And all that will remain
Is this little house, in this little town,

And my prayers
Where God takes an invocation and sews a universe,
But not for me.
For I will remain
In the garden of here and now.

My Lady

Death is a drug, and time is sobriety.
Inside the wind is a mockery.
But there is only one moment when the soul
is taken by an angel.
And peace, peace be upon you, it says.
I am a willow, drowning in the sunlight.
I am a wasted moment
Damning the star above to burn for eternity.
And I am the only respite
That a mother can rely on…
The sun shines, a billion years, a breath of
space,
And then, black hole.

Abecedarian

Ah, I'm a follower of the
Born again
Christ.
Death and solitude are
Everlasting.
Follow me to the
Godhead,
Here I am,
I am here, alone amongst the cherry trees.
Just because I am a woman,
Kind and fertile,
Loneliness follows me to the end.
My whole being is a nubile root,
Over the soil,
Pregnant with rain.
Que signifie la dette de la mort?
Rien.
Soldiers think of me,
Taking in my beauty.
Under the soil,
Very pregnant with damp water,
Water.
Xylotomies of my flesh,
Yes, they study,
Zealous of my autopsy.

The Fall

Until sun and moon rise with the dark night,
We will father China.
Until the dust burns our eyes with the sky-
light,
We will find Iran.

Wise holy side, rip my love from the equato-
rial mist.
Longing for a mascot,
A sun,
A nightly shackle to hold the criminal mark
That berates us, those who
Take, bind, and fall for love.

Only I can hold the mirror.
It reflects the beauty of a narrator.
Weeds populate this quarter.
I have never been in love except
With the enemy.

Mercy, time, all that speaks.
Mint and war, sigh with the time bomb.

Together we relate,
Without the skies to guide me.

What will the heavenly sighs widen inside
my moaning sun?
The heavens say, "We are mindless and emp-
ty."
We are the umbilical softness of youth and
time.

Must we believe in God to become
The dying race of ethereal might?

Yes. But chide the skies with doubt,
And you will find us, reckoning with dia-
monds.

When Winter Comes to Me

I sway with winding currents in the sunlit
sigh.
Wishing you would let me miles away, burn.

I belong to the secrets of misery and love.
Mercy, they hold it from me.

I boldly burn the winter's life.
I know a song that sang the hummingbird
last spring.

I had to watch nature blind its ferns with the
dust of man's birth.
Winter, love me.
Take my shadow and cast it underneath the
burdened lakes.

The city grinds.
It grinds with tectonic life.

Meet me in the Garden of Eden.
We will share our lives under painted memo-
ries of the world.

Life is ending. I know, you know.

Peace

When did peace live in the winds of Andalu-
sia?
Nay, they bring me to the edge of a sad lone
fiend.
Hopeless and forever, the lies are abound.

Fatherless and limp, the gestation period of
creation
Is water.
Lo, the winter is here.
Forever is my name.

There came to him an angel.
And this is the story.
And this is the story.
However, they break you.
And they sigh on the day you were born.
Never become the end.

Because, I will see you in heaven,
And you will be the age of reason.
Blight and fortune are one.

Like a dream.

The Sky

Whenever the sky rips with thunder,
I rejoice in the matrimony of
The fertile earth and wind and rain.

Together we will force God to create
A new man.

Cogito

The sole reason for existence is to wander the
mind.
If the mind exists, cogito, hum.

I realized yesterday that love was for me.
And through the eye, the eye. Windows of
the
Soul of the dogwood.

I have learned to love another.
And though you remain, I ponder the sky's
reasoning.
Thick with dew, my soft eyes.

This remnant of a sorrow, so weak, so many
minds.

Maybe once I was the fragrance of the water
lily,
But, no, I have taken you to be a friend.

And the lofty heights of Saturn rise...
...under the furthest heaven.

Wild Fauna

Darkness and the ability to cry
Into the night, like an animal
Howls and the bird calls to his mate,
This is the philosophy of modern man.

Coup

The weeds plot the downfall of the lily.
Insomuch as a dark moan,
They are strangled, force, vital force.

It is said that Monday weeps for the weary.
And when the tears choke me, a blind scare.
The ignorant widely rebuke the softness of all
that is one.

The force of flora and fauna, the forever to be
stopped.
The infinite ability to love,
And the fertility of the earth's last days.

Yes, monuments will be constructed
To remember the foreign wars.
But the East is volcanic,

The West a fury of hunger.
This is the minute I request to detail my
thoughts:
I became the wide eyed maid, and dreamed
that

So many days would number this tiny life.
And I will be mistaken
At the prophecy of wind.

Stolen Light

Stolen light, like a light-gone, light-dead,
Fatherless and numb. Flight like dying death
like love.
Mint is the essence of the earthly tide.

Like angels circling, circling the globe.
Hide the stars, hide them.
I will find a moonstone and wear the jeweled
sky.

Beauty is formed.
It's silent, it's sad and little.
But love, water lily, love me, love the end of
time.

Silent lover, silhouette of the night.
Ancient. Ancient life, a path of fathers,
Trail of kin, genetic life, burning in the blood.

Wheel ! Turning. Around
The fate of the clock.
Ticking time, no time, no space.

Finish me,

I will find a way to you here.
So meet nothing in the starry skies.

I'll be here for a little while.

Untitled 7

15,000,000 sands
14 skies
I had morning in my blood, and mass, love
behold me

Man, I'm war, with your mass

Hemlock

hemlock
it's hemlock
haven't you seen a light ?
it's water lily

Amongst Lovers

Inside the wind, a mockery.
A lone song, sung.
Mute is the willow,
Mind is the fawn.

I nod to sleep inside the wide acreage of woe.
When, when will the yarrow bind us togeth-
er?
Until the solemn age has begun,
The lightning rung for softness.

I want to find a seal,
A fine addition to my home.
Finite light, never leave me.

I'm foreign in a land of winds.
I'm witched, remorseful.

Time is the essence of suns.
Moving and swaying
To your unbelief.

Little do you know of innocence
And heart.

I Am a Child

Call out to me when you are lost at sea
And I will remember you as you take
Your last breath.

And perhaps I will deliver you to the shore,
Like Jonah, who lost the world of worlds.

The World of Probability

We have come so far for rain,
The multiplied rewards for hardship and work.
And science beckons my mind,
To the world of thought and experience.

My lover hides mathematical genius in his hair.
And I am the wind, rustling beneath the trees,
Low and unforgiving, foreboding and distressed.

My mind tells me I'm just a calculation of the godhead,
And a number in the world of chance.

Hope in a Prayer

I, inhaling smoke from the mist of time,
Am reverberating over the hills of decay and loss.
I am a white horse,
Running from my destiny.
I am a small child,
Hope in a prayer.

Do you know a light?
It's the star, so distant and forlorn without an earth to give life to.
And so small to your deep eyes.

Take me, finish me.
Meet nothing in the starry skies, where lovers meet for eternity.
Take this finite life, and finish me.

The Hill

I have climbed this hill,
For the view of a setting sun.
It hurts my eyes to see beauty.
I'm standing in the wind,
Among the clover patch,
And I'm remembering when I was once the lily of the valley.
I was once that fragrance, that fertile womb where death overtook me.

Now I'm on this hill,
And the sun, setting, knows nothing of my pain, or of my grief.
It only knows it's life force, vital force, the sustainer of violence and energy.

The Howling Wind

Oh, I theorize about your eyes
And dark gaze.
How wind sways to your disbelief.
And me, taking refuge in religion.

And I wonder:

...my incantations mute under a howling
moon.

A Land

Oh, I'm rich, a mineral feast.
Plant the white lily in my long flowing hair.
Bring me to your mother's grave.
Bring me home.

I have taken the road towards love,
But I got lost inside your eyes.
Your eyes, a gaze of power and desire.

I'm a girl, from no man's land.
No one will be looking for me,
So let me migrate
To a place where the tyrant is no longer in
me.

A Moniker

There, a moniker.
I'm whispering so soft a prayer to the unknown.
I'm a seer, they say in the East. And a burden in the West.

But time is so fluid these days.
It's so funny. They laugh when I say matter doesn't exist.
Unknown bible of the broken cross.
Unknown lover of the wayward past.

I'm seeing my angel in a dream, like light
dancing on a prison wall.

The Wind of Yesterday

I am a dark winter that huddles for
warmth
At the quaking of the sea.

Into the Night

There is music in the crickets,
And mathematics in nature, they say.
But I believe in chaos and the wild
Birthing of skies.

The Orchid

This morning was the dew's epiphany.
The sigh of dawn, the crashing of the day.
Sun's rise, and following a path, the day be-
gan.

This trite and formidable phenomenon,
Hollow.
And remember me, dear, as the noon begins
its charade.

Hum with the sacred hour.
It's time that forgets the years.
And remark the path of the sun.

It's wide and unbearable. But, oh, the orchid
begs to differ.

The Old Meadow

Where I lay my head is a sea,
Of grass and hope.
Together we relate to the sky with jaded
fury
Of our destiny, the winter's prolongment.

My Heart, a Political Motion

I am taken by the votes that sway
Into the current of the population.
We have spoken of time passing.
And we have gifted the nation
With the freedom of the globe.

Acknowledgments

Thank you to Charlotte Steigenga and David Cope.

www.ingramcontent.com/pod-product-compliance
Lightning Source LLC
LaVergne TN
LVHW052106160826
845678LV00015B/3383

* 9 7 9 8 8 4 0 8 4 4 7 3 1 *